The Witch's Year

MODERN MAGIC
IN 52 CARDS

Clare Gogerty

A Year of Modern Magic

Have you ever looked at a full moon on a clear winter night and shivered? Or sown a seed and marvelled as it unfurled from the earth? Have you walked in an ancient forest or sat in a stone circle and felt a deep sense of peace and belonging? Do you wonder if there is something beyond the grind of the everyday? Do you believe in magic?

If the answer to any of these questions is yes, then you need witchcraft in your life. No longer tainted by notions of sorcery, hexes and cobwebs, witchcraft has been rediscovered by those of us yearning for re-enchantment. Another way of looking at the world opens up when we take time to cast a spell, interpret the tarot, honour our ancestors with rituals or watch our pendulums swing – a new perspective filled with mystery, wonder and possibility.

How to Use the Cards

These cards will guide you through a year of magic. Based on the cycles of nature and guided by the seasons, they will give you the tools and know-how to unveil the magic that surrounds us. By celebrating the eight sabbats (festivals) of the Wheel of the Year, you will work with nature to activate your hidden power and trigger miraculous happenings. Witchcraft can attract love, give your career a boost, protect your home and help with healing. It will enrich your life. Whether you are a solitary hedge witch or part of a coven, a practising witch or an aspiring one, this book will take you on a year-long magical adventure. Work by selecting the current sabbat, then choose your spell, ritual or exercise from one of those cards.

Working with the Four Elements

The four elements of earth, air, fire and water are the basis of all life on the planet. They are also the foundation of natural magic and central to spell work and rituals. Each element corresponds to an astrological sign, season, colour and cardinal direction (also called a 'quarter'). Tools used in magic work are assigned to different elements; the governing element is used to purify the tool before magic work begins.

▽ Earth

Direction: north
Meaning: material abundance, fertility, work, money
Season: winter
Astrological signs: Taurus, Virgo, Capricorn
Colours: green, gold, black
Tool: the pentagram

△ Fire

Direction: south
Meaning: inspiration, intuition, creativity, sexual energy
Season: summer
Astrological signs: Leo, Sagittarius, Aries
Colours: orange, red
Tool: the athame

△ Air

Direction: east
Meaning: intellect, clarity of thought, communication
Season: spring
Astrological signs: Aquarius, Libra, Gemini
Colour: yellow
Tool: the wand

▽ Water

Direction: west
Meaning: emotions, love, psychic power
Season: Autumn
Astrological signs: Scorpio, Pisces, Cancer
Colours: blue, silver
Tool: the cauldron

The Wheel of the Year

The natural world is at the heart of witchcraft. Witches observe and respond to the seasons and cycles of nature and are guided by its wisdom. The eight chapters in this book correspond to the eight annual sabbats of the witch's calendar. These occur at equal intervals throughout the year and mark the high point of the seasons and moments in the agricultural calendar. Originally Celtic festivals, they occur at solar events called solstices and equinoxes and at the midpoints between them.

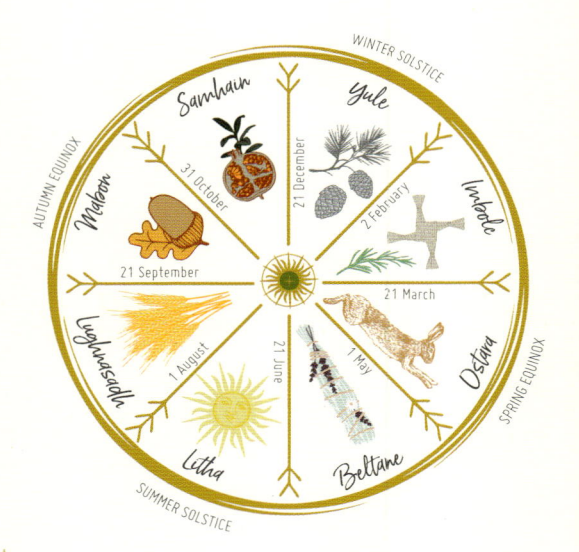

On a sabbat, witches honour gods, goddesses and nature, and are thankful for all that they provide. As well as a time of ritual and reflection, sabbats are a good opportunity to eat and drink with other witches. Some chose to gather in covens, although many witches choose to practise alone.

The cycle of the eight sabbats is called the Wheel of the Year and is the cosmic cycle of all things: birth followed by death, then renewal. Picture the sabbats as the eight spokes on a wheel, constantly turning as surely as night follows day and summer follows winter.

Two of the eight sabbats occur at solstices (the longest and the shortest day) and two at equinoxes (when day and night are of equal length). These are the solar, or minor, sabbats, which are also known as quarter days. In the midpoints between them are the four Earth, or major, sabbats, which are also known as cross-quarter days.

The Eight Sabbats

The dates for the eight sabbats in the northern hemisphere are given below. In the Southern Hemisphere, some witches follow the traditional northern hemisphere wheel. For example, they celebrate Samhain in October. However, it can be difficult to prepare for the harvest sabbat when it is early spring. As a result, other witches work harmoniously with the cycles of nature and celebrate sabbats during the appropriate season.

The word 'sabbat', meaning the witch's festival, is based on a claim made by Gerald Gardner, an English witch and anthropologist. He suggested that the word was first used in the Middle Ages and was a mixture of the Jewish Shabbat and other heretical celebrations.

The four major sabbats

Samhain *31 October*
The witch's year begins. Plants die back, dead souls return. A time to prepare to descend into stillness.

Imbolc *2 February*
The darkest days are over; the earth is preparing to burst into life.

Beltane *1 May*
A festival of fertility. Plants sprout rapid external growth. A time of development and learning.

Lughnasadh *1 August*
The first harvest. Plants are fruiting. A time to be grateful for what has been created.

The four minor sabbats

The two solstices mark the turning points of the year.

Winter solstice (Yule), *21 December*: the shortest day. Plants are dormant. This is a time of stillness, rest and recuperation.

Summer solstice (Litha), *21 June*: the longest day. A time of intense, active energy and powerful magic.

The two equinoxes occur when the sun passes across the equator, making night and day equal across the globe.

Spring/Vernal equinox (Ostara), *21 March*: the first day of spring. Germination begins. A time of powerful energetic release.

Autumn equinox (Mabon), *21 September*: the second harvest. Seeds are dispersed. A time to take responsibility for our actions.

What a Witch Needs:
tools to make your magic fly

You do not need to spend a fortune to perform magic, but spell casting and rituals are much more effective with the right tools, and there are a few items that are essential. Most of these can be home-made or adapted from things you already own.

Altar

This is central to all that you do as a witch, so take a little time to set it up and decorate it. Find a place in your home where the altar will not be disturbed. This could be a mantelpiece, windowsill, shelf or a simple raised structure on a table. You do not have to buy anything special (unless you want to!); this will be your place of quiet contemplation and ritual, not a display to impress your friends. Some witches place their altars facing north – the realm of midnight, dreams and magic. Others place it facing east to honour the rising sun.

Now to decorate it... Start with your altar cloth (natural fibres like cotton or velvet work well), then add items that chime with the seasons and your intentions – you will find suggestions throughout this book. Candles, crystals and a pentacle are a good selection to start, then you can add flowers, herbs, charms – whatever feels right.

Cauldron

One of the most potent symbols of witchcraft, a cauldron, is also very handy. This round, black pot with three legs and a handle was once a common sight in homes. Hung over a fire, it was used to cook soups, broths and stews. The modern witch has a specially made cauldron, about the size of a medium saucepan, to mix herbal potions, burn incense and cast spells. It is also a lovely thing: the three legs represent the triple goddess and its full-bodied shape symbolizes Mother Earth. Cauldrons have been replaced with saucepans for cooking, and you could use one of these at a push, but they do lack magic. A cauldron is one thing worth investing in.

Athame

Pronounced a-thay-me, this is the witch's ritual knife. Never used for cutting (except for the cake at a hand-fasting ceremony), it is used to direct and control psychic energy, to draw magic circles and to call the quarters (point to the four cardinal directions) at the start of your rituals. Traditionally, an athame was made of silver or steel, with a black wooden handle. Some have double edges and are decorated with symbols and runes. It is important to treat your athame with respect. Purify and consecrate it before rituals, then wrap it in a white cloth and keep in a safe place when it is not being used.

Wand

Made from wood taken from a sacred tree, a wand is used to send a spell in whatever direction the wand is pointed. Wands made from different trees have different purposes: hazel or elder make good all-round magic wands; apple wood works in love spells, and willow is good for working with lunar energies.

Crystals

Stones have long been credited with magical and healing properties, especially glittering semi-precious stones that seem to radiate inner light or flash with iridescent colours. Either quarried or appearing magically on the surface of the earth, the range and beauty of these gems is incredible and varied. They have been used for thousands of years, their magical and spiritual power harnessed as amulets to ward off evil, to bring the wearer good luck or to cure various ailments.

The modern witch uses crystals and stones to complement their magical work, either placed on the altar, worn as jewellery, incorporated into a wand or simply carried in a pocket. Held in the hand during meditation, the right crystal will help you focus and keep you grounded. Some witches also use crystals to heal themselves or others, either spiritually or physically. Although there is no evidence to show that crystal healing works and it is not a form of medicine, more and more people are open to trying the possible benefits that crystals bring.

Pentagram

This five-pointed star, the most important symbol for a witch, is a core element of witchcraft. The four lower points represent the four elements, with the uppermost point representing the fifth element: spirit. The pentagram also resembles the human form, with the head at the top and four limbs extending from the central 'body'.

Place a pentagram at the centre of your altar and have it nearby during spell work. Either draw one on a piece of paper or buy a more substantial metal or ceramic version. Before use, cleanse and charge it overnight in the light of the full moon. When a pentagram is enclosed in a circle, it is called a pentacle. This disc is often worn by modern witches as protective jewellery and to identify themselves to other witches.

Incense

Incense is a blend of resins, herbs, spices and oils that releases a powerful aroma when burned. It creates the right atmosphere for spell work, depending on the ingredients chosen.

Candles

The gentle light of a candle creates a calm, focused mood that will give your spells and rituals weight and potency. Lighting a candle is a sacred gesture, summoning the elements of fire and air and symbolizing the light that is born out of darkness. It's a good idea to have a selection of candles in a variety of colours and sizes. Differently coloured candles have different meanings: pink is used for love spells, silver for clairvoyance, green to bring abundance, blue for healing and inspiration, and purple for protection. White is a neutral colour and can be used for anything. Use a fresh candle for each spell and allow it to burn down and extinguish after magic work (shorter candles or tea lights are a safer option as they burn out faster).

Book of Shadows

Recording all your witchy activities in a book is a satisfying and useful thing to do. A type of supernatural journal, a book of shadows (also known as a grimoire) is an important map of your witch's journey. Use it to write up all your spells, rituals, incantations, herbal remedies and incense recipes.

Do not be tempted to record all of this on a computer: it needs to be hand-written, preferably in blue ink. Keep your book of shadows safe, and remember to update it. It is an essential tool and a record of how far you have come.

A Witch's Herbal

Using plants, especially herbs, in spells and remedies is an important part of the witch's repertoire. Herbal magic is known as 'wortcunning' ('wort' means 'plant' and 'cunning' means 'knowledge') and draws on the healing and magical properties of plants.

Plants, trees and herbs embody magical qualities that resonate at different times of the year. Those that work well with certain seasons and sabbats are recommended in the relevant chapter of this book, but do not feel restricted – work with them whenever it feels right.

Crystal Magic

Stones have long been credited with magical and healing properties, especially glittering semi-precious stones that seem to radiate inner light or flash with iridescent colours. Either quarried or appearing magically on the surface of the earth, the range and beauty is incredible and varied.

Crystals have been used for thousands of years, their magical and spiritual power harnessed as amulets to ward off evil, to bring the wearer good luck or to cure various ailments.

The modern witch uses crystals and stones to complement their magical work, either placed on the altar, worn as jewellery, incorporated into a wand or simply carried in a pocket. Held in the hand during meditation, the right crystal will help you focus and keep you grounded.

Casting a Spell

Even with the advent of technology and advances in science, more and more of us are placing our faith in acts of magic. Belief in spells has been with us since ancient times, with methods varying according to faith system and culture. At the heart of spell making, and common to all beliefs, is a simple plea to make things better. This is communicated to a chosen deity by speech or a written note and accompanied by a ritual. Similar to prayer, a spell is a way to focus the mind, strengthen the will and ask for help. And it can be amazingly effective.

The ethics of spell working

The power of spells can be harnessed to do harm as well as good. To avoid damaging anyone or anything, it is important to have the right intention and to choose the right words before casting a spell. Follow these guidelines and you cannot go wrong:

✳ Never work to harm anyone.
✳ Never work to manipulate anyone against their will.
✳ Never work for your own gain at someone else's expense.
✳ Word your spell carefully so you do not break any of these rules.
✳ For extra caution, end the spell with "and may this spell work for the greatest good of all."

How to cast a spell

This is just one way to do spell work; there are no hard-and-fast rules. Think of it as an outline, and add extra elements and embellishments as you see fit. There are other spells throughout the book, which you can work with and adapt where necessary. Always do what feels right for you.

1. Make sure you are somewhere you are unlikely to be disturbed, then set the scene: dim the lights and burn incense that corresponds with your intention for the spell.

2. Add items to your altar that fit your mood. Light a candle or two, choosing coloured ones that complement your purpose.

3. Draw a magic circle either by walking around its circumference or drawing it in the air with your athame or wand.

4. State the purpose of your spell, either speaking it out loud, writing it on a piece of paper or both. Choose a deity or spirit guide to assist you. This could be your favourite deity or one that fits the spell, or simply put in a request to the universe.

5. Repeat your chosen incantation several times. As you say it, focus your mind and visualize the outcome. Concentrate.

6. With your wand, direct the spell out into the universe towards its goal.

7. Thank your chosen deity.

8. Unwind the circle and wait for the magic to manifest.

About the author

Clare lives on a smallholding in rural Herefordshire, which she intends to open as a spiritual retreat. The sound of shamanic drumming often comes from her orchard where she has built a stone labyrinth, and herbal remedies are frequently cooked up in the kitchen. She has been interested in magic, folklore and Druidry since childhood, and is often on an adventure to find standing stones or an ancient path. Find her on Instagram: **@waysidewitch**

A former magazine editor, Clare is now a freelance journalist and author, writing about spirituality and travel for various magazines and newspapers. In 2019, her book *Beyond the Footpath: mindful adventures for modern pilgrims* was published, followed by *Sacred Places: where to find wonder in the world* in 2020.

A David and Charles Publication

© David and Charles, Ltd 2021

David and Charles is an imprint of David and Charles, Ltd
Suite A, Tourism House, Pynes Hill, Exeter, EX2 5WS

Text and Designs © Clare Gogerty 2021
Layout and Illustrations © David and Charles, Ltd 2021

First published in the UK and USA in 2021 as
The Witch's Yearbook: Spells, Stones, Tools and Rituals for a Year of Modern Magic.

The authors and the publisher have made every effort to ensure that all the instructions are accurate and safe, and therefore cannot accept liability for any resulting injury, damage, or loss to persons or property, however it may arise.

David and Charles is an imprint of David and Charles, Ltd
Suite A, Tourism House, Pynes Hill, Exeter, EX2 5WS

FSC
www.fsc.org
MIX
Paper from responsible sources
FSC® C020056

David and Charles publishes high-quality books and gifts on a wide range of subjects.

For more information visit **www.davidandcharles.com**.

DAVID & CHARLES